PARADISE LOST

BOOK-I

John Milton

Published by

Hawk Press
4836/24, Ansari Road, Daryaganj
New Delhi – 110 002
Phones: +91-11-23278618, +91-11-43667199
E-mail: thehawkpress@gmail.com
www.thehawkpress.com

BOOK-I

Of Mans First Disobedience, and the Fruit
Of that Forbidden Tree, whose mortal tast
Brought Death into the World, and all our woe,
With loss of Eden, till one greater Man
Restore us, and regain the blissful Seat,
Sing Heav'nly Muse, that on the secret top
Of Oreb, or of Sinai, didst inspire
That Shepherd, who first taught the chosen Seed,
In the Beginning how the Heav'ns and Earth
Rose out of Chaos: Or if Sion Hill
Delight thee more, and Siloa's Brook that flow'd
Fast by the Oracle of God; I thence
Invoke thy aid to my adventrous Song,
That with no middle flight intends to soar
Above th' Aonian Mount, while it pursues
Things unattempted yet in Prose or Rhime.
And chiefly Thou O Spirit, that dost prefer
Before all Temples th' upright heart and pure,
Instruct me, for Thou know'st; Thou from the first
Wast present, and with mighty wings outspread

Dove-like satst brooding on the vast Abyss
And mad'st it pregnant: What in me is dark
Illumine, what is low raise and support;
That to the highth of this great Argument
I may assert th' Eternal Providence,
And justifie the wayes of God to men.
    Say first, for Heav'n hides nothing from thy view
Nor the deep Tract of Hell, say first what cause
Mov'd our Grand Parents in that happy State,
Favour'd of Heav'n so highly, to fall off
From their Creator, and transgress his Will
For one restraint, Lords of the World besides?
Who first seduc'd them to that fowl revolt?
Th' infernal Serpent; he it was, whose guile
Stird up with Envy and Revenge, deceiv'd
The Mother of Mankinde, what time his Pride
Had cast him out from Heav'n, with all his Host
Of Rebel Angels, by whose aid aspiring
To set himself in Glory above his Peers,
He trusted to have equal'd the most High,
If he oppos'd; and with ambitious aim
Against the Throne and Monarchy of God
Rais'd impious War in Heav'n and Battel proud
With vain attempt. Him the Almighty Power
Hurld headlong flaming from th' Ethereal Skie
With hideous ruine and combustion down
To bottomless perdition, there to dwell

In Adamantine Chains and penal Fire,

Who durst defie th' Omnipotent to Arms.

Nine times the Space that measures Day and Night

To mortal men, he with his horrid crew

Lay vanquisht, rowling in the fiery Gulfe

Confounded though immortal: But his doom

Reserv'd him to more wrath; for now the thought

Both of lost happiness and lasting pain

Torments him; round he throws his baleful eyes

That witness'd huge affliction and dismay

Mixt with obdurate pride and stedfast hate:

At once as far as Angels kenn he views

The dismal Situation waste and wilde,

A Dungeon horrible, on all sides round

As one great Furnace flam'd, yet from those flames

No light, but rather darkness visible

Serv'd only to discover sights of woe,

Regions of sorrow, doleful shades, where peace

And rest can never dwell, hope never comes

That comes to all; but torture without end

Still urges, and a fiery Deluge, fed

With ever-burning Sulphur unconsum'd:

Such place Eternal Justice had prepar'd

For those rebellious, here their Prison ordain'd

In utter darkness, and their portion set

As far remov'd from God and light of Heav'n

As from the Center thrice to th' utmost Pole.

O how unlike the place from whence they fell!

There the companions of his fall, o'rewhelm'd

With Floods and Whirlwinds of tempestuous fire,

He soon discerns, and weltring by his side

One next himself in power, and next in crime,

Long after known in Palestine, and nam'd

Beelzebub. To whom th' Arch-Enemy,

And thence in Heav'n call'd Satan, with bold words

Breaking the horrid silence thus began.

    If thou beest he; But O how fall'n! how chang'd

From him, who in the happy Realms of Light

Cloth'd with transcendent brightnes didst outshine

Myriads though bright: If he whom mutual league,

United thoughts and counsels, equal hope,

And hazard in the Glorious Enterprize,

Joynd with me once, now misery hath joynd

In equal ruin: into what Pit thou seest

From what highth fal'n, so much the stronger provd

He with his Thunder: and till then who knew

The force of those dire Arms? yet not for those

Nor what the Potent Victor in his rage

Can else inflict do I repent or change,

Though chang'd in outward lustre; that fixt mind

And high disdain, from sence of injur'd merit,

That with the mightiest rais'd me to contend,

And to the fierce contention brought along

Innumerable force of Spirits arm'd

That durst dislike his reign, and me preferring,

His utmost power with adverse power oppos'd

In dubious Battel on the Plains of Heav'n,

And shook his throne. What though the field be lost?

All is not lost; the unconquerable Will,

And study of revenge, immortal hate,

And courage never to submit or yield:

And what is else not to be overcome?

That Glory never shall his wrath or might

Extort from me. To bow and sue for grace

With suppliant knee, and deifie his power

Who from the terrour of this Arm so late

Doubted his Empire, that were low indeed,

That were an ignominy and shame beneath

This downfall; since by Fate the strength of Gods

And this Empyreal substance cannot fail,

Since through experience of this great event

In Arms not worse, in foresight much advanc't,

We may with more successful hope resolve

To wage by force or guile eternal Warr

Irreconcileable, to our grand Foe,

Who now triumphs, and in th' excess of joy

Sole reigning holds the Tyranny of Heav'n.

　　So spake th' Apostate Angel, though in pain,

Vaunting aloud, but rackt with deep despare:

And him thus answer'd soon his bold Compeer.

　　O Prince, O Chief of many Throned Powers,

That led th' imbattelld Seraphim to Warr
Under thy conduct, and in dreadful deeds
Fearless, endanger'd Heav'ns perpetual King;
And put to proof his high Supremacy,
Whether upheld by strength, or Chance, or Fate,
Too well I see and rue the dire event,
That with sad overthrow and foul defeat
Hath lost us Heav'n, and all this mighty Host
In horrible destruction laid thus low,
As far as Gods and Heav'nly Essences
Can Perish: for the mind and spirit remains
Invincible, and vigour soon returns,
Though all our Glory extinct, and happy state
Here swallow'd up in endless misery.
But what if he our Conquerour, (whom I now
Of force believe Almighty, since no less
Then such could hav orepow'rd such force as ours)
Have left us this our spirit and strength intire
Strongly to suffer and support our pains,
That we may so suffice his vengeful ire,
Or do him mightier service as his thralls
By right of Warr, what e're his business be
Here in the heart of Hell to work in Fire,
Or do his Errands in the gloomy Deep;
What can it then avail though yet we feel
Strength undiminisht, or eternal being
To undergo eternal punishment?

Whereto with speedy words th' Arch-fiend reply'd.

   Fall'n Cherube, to be weak is miserable

Doing or Suffering: but of this be sure,

To do ought good never will be our task,

But ever to do ill our sole delight,

As being the contrary to his high will

Whom we resist. If then his Providence

Out of our evil seek to bring forth good,

Our labour must be to pervert that end,

And out of good still to find means of evil;

Which oft times may succeed, so as perhaps

Shall grieve him, if I fail not, and disturb

His inmost counsels from their destind aim.

But see the angry Victor hath recall'd

His Ministers of vengeance and pursuit

Back to the Gates of Heav'n: The Sulphurous Hail

Shot after us in storm, oreblown hath laid

The fiery Surge, that from the Precipice

Of Heav'n receiv'd us falling, and the Thunder,

Wing'd with red Lightning and impetuous rage,

Perhaps hath spent his shafts, and ceases now

To bellow through the vast and boundless Deep.

Let us not slip th' occasion, whether scorn,

 Or satiate fury yield it from our Foe.

Seest thou yon dreary Plain, forlorn and wilde,

 The seat of desolation, voyd of light,

Save what the glimmering of these livid flames

Casts pale and dreadful? Thither let us tend
From off the tossing of these fiery waves,
There rest, if any rest can harbour there,
And reassembling our afflicted Powers,
Consult how we may henceforth most offend
Our Enemy, our own loss how repair,
How overcome this dire Calamity,
What reinforcement we may gain from Hope,
If not what resolution from despare.

    Thus Satan talking to his neerest Mate
With Head up-lift above the wave, and Eyes
That sparkling blaz'd, his other Parts besides
Prone on the Flood, extended long and large
Lay floating many a rood, in bulk as huge
As whom the Fables name of monstrous size,
Titanian, or Earth-born, that warr'd on Jove,
Briarios or Typhon, whom the Den
By ancient Tarsus held, or that Sea-beast
Leviathan, which God of all his works
Created hugest that swim th' Ocean stream:
Him haply slumbring on the Norway foam
The Pilot of some small night-founder'd Skiff,
Deeming some Island, oft, as Sea-men tell,
With fixed Anchor in his skaly rind
Moors by his side under the Lee, while Night
Invests the Sea, and wished Morn delayes:
So stretcht out huge in length the Arch-fiend lay

Chain'd on the burning Lake, nor ever thence
Had ris'n or heav'd his head, but that the will
And high permission of all-ruling Heaven
Left him at large to his own dark designs,
That with reiterated crimes he might
Heap on himself damnation, while he sought
Evil to others, and enrag'd might see
How all his malice serv'd but to bring forth
Infinite goodness, grace and mercy shewn
On Man by him seduc't, but on himself
Treble confusion, wrath and vengeance pour'd.
Forthwith upright he rears from off the Pool
His mighty Stature; on each hand the flames
Drivn backward slope their pointing spires, & rowld
In billows, leave i'th' midst a horrid Vale.
Then with expanded wings he stears his flight
Aloft, incumbent on the dusky Air
That felt unusual weight, till on dry Land
He lights, if it were Land that ever burn'd
With solid, as the Lake with liquid fire;
And such appear'd in hue, as when the force
Of subterranean wind transports a Hill
Torn from Pelorus, or the shatter'd side
Of thundring Aetna, whose combustible
And fewel'd entrals thence conceiving Fire,
Sublim'd with Mineral fury, aid the Winds,
And leave a singed bottom all involv'd

With stench and smoak: Such resting found the sole

Of unblest feet. Him followed his next Mate,

Both glorying to have scap't the Stygian flood

As Gods, and by their own recover'd strength,

Not by the sufferance of supernal Power.

        Is this the Region, this the Soil, the Clime,

Said then the lost Arch Angel, this the seat

That we must change for Heav'n, this mournful gloom

For that celestial light? Be it so, since hee

Who now is Sovran can dispose and bid

What shall be right: fardest from him is best

Whom reason hath equald, force hath made supream

Above his equals. Farewel happy Fields

Where Joy for ever dwells: Hail horrours, hail

Infernal world, and thou profoundest Hell

Receive thy new Possessor: One who brings

A mind not to be chang'd by Place or Time.

The mind is its own place, and in it self

Can make a Heav'n of Hell, a Hell of Heav'n.

What matter where, if I be still the same,

And what I should be, all but less then hee

Whom Thunder hath made greater? Here at least

We shall be free; th' Almighty hath not built

Here for his envy, will not drive us hence:

Here we may reign secure, and in my choyce

To reign is worth ambition though in Hell:

Better to reign in Hell, then serve in Heav'n.

But wherefore let we then our faithful friends,

Th' associates and copartners of our loss

Lye thus astonisht on th' oblivious Pool,

And call them not to share with us their part

In this unhappy Mansion, or once more

With rallied Arms to try what may be yet

Regaind in Heav'n, or what more lost in Hell?

   So Satan spake, and him Beelzebub

Thus answer'd. Leader of those Armies bright,

Which but th' Omnipotent none could have foyld,

If once they hear that voyce, their liveliest pledge

Of hope in fears and dangers, heard so oft

In worst extreams, and on the perilous edge

Of battel when it rag'd, in all assaults

Their surest signal, they will soon resume

New courage and revive, though now they lye

Groveling and prostrate on yon Lake of Fire,

As we erewhile, astounded and amaz'd,

No wonder, fall'n such a pernicious highth.

   He scarce had ceas't when the superiour Fiend

Was moving toward the shore; his ponderous shield

Ethereal temper, massy, large and round,

Behind him cast; the broad circumference

Hung on his shoulders like the Moon, whose Orb

Through Optic Glass the Tuscan Artist views

At Ev'ning from the top of Fesole,

Or in Valdarno, to descry new Lands,

Rivers or Mountains in her spotty Globe.

His Spear, to equal which the tallest Pine

Hewn on Norwegian hills, to be the Mast

Of some great Ammiral, were but a wand,

He walkt with to support uneasie steps

Over the burning Marle, not like those steps

On Heavens Azure, and the torrid Clime

Smote on him sore besides, vaulted with Fire;

Nathless he so endur'd, till on the Beach

Of that inflamed Sea, he stood and call'd

His Legions, Angel Forms, who lay intrans't

Thick as Autumnal Leaves that strow the Brooks

In Vallombrosa, where th' Etrurian shades

High overarch't imbowr; or scatterd sedge

Afloat, when with fierce Winds Orion arm'd

Hath vext the Red-Sea Coast, whose waves orethrew

Busiris and his Memphian Chivalrie,

VVhile with perfidious hatred they pursu'd

The Sojourners of Goshen, who beheld

From the safe shore their floating Carkases

And broken Chariot Wheels, so thick bestrown

Abject and lost lay these, covering the Flood,

Under amazement of their hideous change.

He call'd so loud, that all the hollow Deep

Of Hell resounded. Princes, Potentates,

Warriers, the Flowr of Heav'n, once yours, now lost,

If such astonishment as this can sieze

Eternal spirits; or have ye chos'n this place
After the toyl of Battel to repose
Your wearied vertue, for the ease you find
To slumber here, as in the Vales of Heav'n?
Or in this abject posture have ye sworn
To adore the Conquerour? who now beholds
Cherube and Seraph rowling in the Flood
With scatter'd Arms and Ensigns, till anon
His swift pursuers from Heav'n Gates discern
Th' advantage, and descending tread us down
Thus drooping, or with linked Thunderbolts
Transfix us to the bottom of this Gulfe.
Awake, arise, or be for ever fall'n.
    They heard, and were abasht, and up they sprung
Upon the wing, as when men wont to watch
On duty, sleeping found by whom they dread,
Rouse and bestir themselves ere well awake.
Nor did they not perceave the evil plight
In which they were, or the fierce pains not feel;
Yet to their Generals Voyce they soon obeyd
Innumerable. As when the potent Rod
Of Amrams Son in Egypts evill day
Wav'd round the Coast, up call'd a pitchy cloud
Of Locusts, warping on the Eastern Wind,
That ore the Realm of impious Pharoah hung
Like Night, and darken'd all the Land of Nile:
So numberless were those bad Angels seen

Hovering on wing under the Cope of Hell

'Twixt upper, nether, and surrounding Fires;

Till, as a signal giv'n, th' uplifted Spear

Of their great Sultan waving to direct

Thir course, in even ballance down they light

On the firm brimstone, and fill all the Plain;

A multitude, like which the populous North

Pour'd never from her frozen loyns, to pass

Rhene or the Danaw, when her barbarous Sons

Came like a Deluge on the South, and spread

Beneath Gibraltar to the Lybian sands.

Forthwith from every Squadron and each Band

The Heads and Leaders thither hast where stood

Their great Commander; Godlike shapes and forms

Excelling human, Princely Dignities,

And Powers that earst in Heaven sat on Thrones;

Though of their Names in heav'nly Records now

Be no memorial, blotted out and ras'd

By thir Rebellion, from the Books of Life.

Nor had they yet among the Sons of Eve

Got them new Names, till wandring ore the Earth,

Through Gods high sufferance for the tryal of man,

By falsities and lyes the greatest part

Of Mankind they corrupted to forsake

God their Creator, and th' invisible

Glory of him, that made them, to transform

Oft to the Image of a Brute, adorn'd

With gay Religions full of Pomp and Gold,

And Devils to adore for Deities:

Then were they known to men by various Names,

And various Idols through the Heathen World.

Say, Muse, their Names then known, who first, who last,

Rous'd from the slumber, on that fiery Couch,

At thir great Emperors call, as next in worth

Came singly where he stood on the bare strand,

While the promiscuous croud stood yet aloof?

The chief were those who from the Pit of Hell

Roaming to seek their prey on earth, durst fix

Their Seats long after next the Seat of God,

Their Altars by his Altar, Gods ador'd

Among the Nations round, and durst abide

Jehovah thundring out of Sion, thron'd

Between the Cherubim; yea, often plac'd

Within his Sanctuary it self their Shrines,

Abominations; and with cursed things

His holy Rites, and solemn Feasts profan'd,

And with their darkness durst affront his light.

First Moloch, horrid King besmear'd with blood

Of human sacrifice, and parents tears,

Though for the noyse of Drums and Timbrels loud

Their childrens cries unheard, that past through fire

To his grim Idol. Him the Ammonite

Worshipt in Rabba and her watry Plain,

In Argob and in Basan, to the stream

Of utmost Arnon. Nor content with such

Audacious neighbourhood, the wisest heart

Of Solomon he led by fraud to build

His Temple right against the Temple of God

On that opprobrious Hill, and made his Grove

The pleasant Vally of Hinnom, Tophet thence

And black Gehenna call'd, the Type of Hell.

Next Chemos, th' obscene dread of Moabs Sons,

From Aroer to Nebo, and the wild

Of Southmost Abarim; in Hesebon

And Heronaim, Seons Realm, beyond

The flowry Dale of Sibma clad with Vines,

And Eleale to th' Asphaltick Pool.

Peor his other Name, when he entic'd

Israel in Sittim on their march from Nile

To do him wanton rites, which cost them woe.

Yet thence his lustful Orgies he enlarg'd

Even to that Hill of scandal, by the Grove

Of Moloch homicide, lust hard by hate;

Till good Josiah drove them thence to Hell.

With these came they, who from the bordring flood

Of old Euphrates to the Brook that parts

Egypt from Syrian ground, had general Names

Of Baalim and Ashtaroth, those male,

These Feminine. For Spirits when they please

Can either Sex assume, or both; so soft

And uncompounded is their Essence pure,

Not ti'd or manacl'd with joynt or limb,

Nor founded on the brittle strength of bones,

Like cumbrous flesh; but in what shape they choose

Dilated or condens't, bright or obscure,

Can execute their aerie purposes,

And works of love or enmity fulfill.

For those the Race of Israel oft forsook

Their living strength, and unfrequented left

His righteous Altar, bowing lowly down

To bestial Gods; for which their heads as low

Bow'd down in Battel, sunk before the Spear

Of despicable foes. With these in troop

Came Astoreth, whom the Phoenicians call'd

Astarte, Queen of Heav'n, with crescent Horns;

To whose bright Image nightly by the Moon

Sidonian Virgins paid their Vows and Songs,

In Sion also not unsung, where stood

Her Temple on th' offensive Mountain, built

By that uxorious King, whose heart though large,

Beguil'd by fair Idolatresses, fell

To Idols foul. Thammuz came next behind,

Whose annual wound in Lebanon allur'd

The Syrian Damsels to lament his fate

In amorous dittyes all a Summers day,

While smooth Adonis from his native Rock

Ran purple to the Sea, suppos'd with blood

Of Thammuz yearly wounded: the Love-tale

Infected Sions daughters with like heat,

Whose wanton passions in the sacred Porch

Ezekiel saw, when by the Vision led

His eye survay'd the dark Idolatries

Of alienated Judah. Next came one

Who mourn'd in earnest, when the Captive Ark

Maim'd his brute Image, head and hands lopt off

In his own Temple, on the grunsel edge,

Where he fell flat, and sham'd his Worshipers:

Dagon his Name, Sea Monster, upward Man

And downward Fish: yet had his Temple high

Rear'd in Azotus, dreaded through the Coast

Of Palestine, in Gath and Ascalon,

And Accaron and Gaza's frontier bounds.

Him follow'd Rimmon, whose delightful Seat

Was fair Damscus, on the fertil Banks

Of Abbana and Pharphar, lucid streams.

He also against the house of God was bold:

A Leper once he lost and gain'd a King,

Ahaz his sottish Conquerour, whom he drew

Gods Altar to disparage and displace

For one of Syrian mode, whereon to burn

His odious offrings, and adore the Gods

Whom he had vanquisht. After these appear'd

A crew who under Names of old Renown,

Osiris, Isis, Orus and their Train

With monstrous shapes and sorceries abus'd

Fanatic Egypt and her Priests, to seek

Thir wandring Gods disguis'd in brutish forms

Rather then human. Nor did Israel scape

Th' infection when their borrow'd Gold compos'd

The Calf in Oreb: and the Rebel King

Doubl'd that sin in Bethel and in Dan,

Lik'ning his Maker to the Grazed Ox,

Jehovah, who in one Night when he pass'd

From Egypt marching, equal'd with one stroke

Both her first born and all her bleating Gods.

Belial came last, then whom a Spirit more lewd

Fell not from Heaven, or more gross to love

Vice for it self: To him no Temple stood

Or Altar smoak'd; yet who more oft then hee

In Temples and at Altars, when the Priest

Turns Atheist, as did Ely's Sons, who fill'd

With lust and violence the house of God.

In Courts and Palaces he also Reigns

And in luxurious Cities, where the noyse

Of riot ascends above thir loftiest Towrs,

And injury and outrage: And when Night

Darkens the Streets, then wander forth the Sons

Of Belial, flown with insolence and wine.

Witness the Streets of Sodom, and that night

In Gibeah, when hospitable Dores

Yielded thir Matrons to prevent worse rape.

These were the prime in order and in might;

The rest were long to tell, though far renown'd,
Th' Ionian Gods, of Javans Issue held
Gods, yet confest later then Heav'n and Earth
Thir boasted Parents; Titan Heav'ns first born
With his enormous brood, and birthright seis'd
By younger Saturn, he from mightier Jove
His own and Rhea's Son like measure found;
So Jove usurping reign'd: these first in Creet
And Ida known, thence on the Snowy top
Of cold Olympus rul'd the middle Air
Thir highest Heav'n; or on the Delphian Cliff,
Or in Dodona, and through all the bounds
Of Doric Land; or who with Saturn old
Fled over Adria to th' Hesperian Fields,
And ore the Celtic roam'd the utmost Isles.
All these and more came flocking; but with looks
Down cast and damp, yet such wherein appear'd
Obscure som glimps of joy, to have found thir chief
Not in despair, to have found themselves not lost
In loss it self; which on his count'nance cast
Like doubtful hue: but he his wonted pride
Soon recollecting, with high words, that bore
Semblance of worth not substance, gently rais'd
Their fainted courage, and dispel'd their fears.
Then strait commands that at the warlike sound
Of Trumpets loud and Clarions be upreard
His mighty Standard; that proud honour claim'd

Azazel as his right, a Cherube tall:
Who forthwith from the glittering Staff unfurld
Th' Imperial Ensign, which full high advanc't
Shon like a Meteor streaming to the Wind
With Gemms and Golden lustre rich imblaz'd,
Seraphic arms and Trophies: all the while
Sonorous mettal blowing Martial sounds:
At which the universal Host upsent
A shout that tore Hells Concave, and beyond
Frighted the Reign of Chaos and old Night.
All in a moment through the gloom were seen
Ten thousand Banners rise into the Air
With Orient Colours waving: with them rose
A Forrest huge of Spears: and thronging Helms
Appear'd, and serried Shields in thick array
Of depth immeasurable: Anon they move
In perfect Phalanx to the Dorian mood
Of Flutes and soft Recorders; such as rais'd
To highth of noblest temper Hero's old
Arming to Battel, and in stead of rage
Deliberate valour breath'd, firm and unmov'd
With dread of death to flight or foul retreat,
Nor wanting power to mitigate and swage
With solemn touches, troubl'd thoughts, and chase
Anguish and doubt and fear and sorrow and pain
From mortal or immortal minds. Thus they
Breathing united force with fixed thought

Mov'd on in silence to soft Pipes that charm'd

Thir painful steps o're the burnt soyle; and now

Advanc't in view they stand, a horrid Front

Of dreadful length and dazling Arms, in guise

Of Warriers old with order'd Spear and Shield,

Awaiting what command thir mighty Chief

Had to impose: He through the armed Files

Darts his experienc't eye, and soon traverse

The whole Battalion views, thir order due,

Thir visages and stature as of Gods,

Thir number last he summs. And now his heart

Distends with pride, and hardning in his strength

Glories: For never since created man,

Met such imbodied force, as nam'd with these

Could merit more then that small infantry

Warr'd on by Cranes: though all the Giant brood

Of Phlegra with th' Heroic Race were joyn'd

That fought at Theb's and Ilium, on each side

Mixt with auxiliar Gods; and what resounds

In Fable or Romance of Uthers Son

Begirt with British and Armoric Knights;

And all who since, Baptiz'd or Infidel

Jousted in Aspramont or Montalban,

Damasco, or Marocco, or Trebisond,

Or whom Biserta sent from Afric shore

When Charlemain with all his Peerage fell

By Fontarabbia. Thus far these beyond

Compare of mortal prowess, yet observ'd

Thir dread Commander: he above the rest

In shape and gesture proudly eminent

Stood like a Towr; his form had yet not lost

All her Original brightness, nor appear'd

Less then Arch Angel ruind, and th' excess

Of Glory obscur'd: As when the Sun new ris'n

Looks through the Horizontal misty Air

Shorn of his Beams, or from behind the Moon

In dim Eclips disastrous twilight sheds

On half the Nations, and with fear of change

Perplexes Monarchs. Dark'n'd so, yet shon

Above them all th' Arch Angel: but his face

Deep scars of Thunder had intrencht, and care

Sat on his faded cheek, but under Browes

Of dauntless courage, and considerate Pride

Waiting revenge: cruel his eye, but cast

Signs of remorse and passion to behold

The fellows of his crime, the followers rather

(Far other once beheld in bliss) condemn'd

For ever now to have their lot in pain,

Millions of Spirits for his fault amerc't

Of Heav'n, and from Eternal Splendors flung

For his revolt, yet faithfull how they stood,

Thir Glory witherd. As when Heavens Fire

Hath scath'd the Forrest Oaks, or Mountain Pines,

With singed top their stately growth though bare

Stands on the blasted Heath. He now prepar'd
To speak; whereat their doubl'd Ranks they bend
From Wing to Wing, and half enclose him round
With all his Peers: attention held them mute.
Thrice he assayd, and thrice in spite of scorn,
Tears such as Angels weep, burst forth: at last
Words interwove with sighs found out their way.

    O Myriads of immortal Spirits, O Powers
Matchless, but with th' Almighty, and that strife
Was not inglorious, though th' event was dire,
As this place testifies, and this dire change
Hateful to utter: but what power of mind
Foreseeing or presaging, from the Depth
Of knowledge past or present, could have fear'd,
How such united force of Gods, how such
As stood like these, could ever know repulse?
For who can yet beleeve, though after loss,
That all these puissant Legions, whose exile
Hath emptied Heav'n, shall faile to re-ascend
Self-rais'd, and repossess their native seat.
For me, be witness all the Host of Heav'n,
If counsels different, or danger shun'd
By me, have lost our hopes. But he who reigns
Monarch in Heav'n, till then as one secure
Sat on his Throne, upheld by old repute,
Consent or custome, and his Regal State
Put forth at full, but still his strength conceal'd,

Which tempted our attempt, and wrought our fall.
Henceforth his might we know, and know our own
So as not either to provoke, or dread
New warr, provok't; our better part remains
To work in close design, by fraud or guile
What force effected not: that he no less
At length from us may find, who overcomes
By force, hath overcome but half his foe.
Space may produce new Worlds; whereof so rife
There went a fame in Heav'n that he ere long
Intended to create, and therein plant
A generation, whom his choice regard
Should favour equal to the Sons of Heaven:
Thither, if but to prie, shall be perhaps
Our first eruption, thither or elsewhere:
For this Infernal Pit shall never hold
Caelestial Spirits in Bondage, nor th' Abysse
Long under darkness cover. But these thoughts
Full Counsel must mature: Peace is despaird,
For who can think Submission? Warr then, Warr
Open or understood must be resolv'd.
     He spake: and to confirm his words, out-flew
Millions of flaming swords, drawn from the thighs
Of mighty Cherubim; the sudden blaze
Far round illumin'd hell: highly they rag'd
Against the Highest, and fierce with grasped arm's
Clash'd on their sounding shields the din of war,

Hurling defiance toward the vault of Heav'n.

    There stood a Hill not far whose griesly top

Belch'd fire and rowling smoak; the rest entire

Shon with a glossie scurff, undoubted sign

That in his womb was hid metallic Ore,

The work of Sulphur. Thither wing'd with speed

A numerous Brigad hasten'd. As when bands

Of Pioners with Spade and Pickaxe arm'd

Forerun the Royal Camp, to trench a Field,

Or cast a Rampart. Mammon led them on,

Mammon, the least erected Spirit that fell

From heav'n, for ev'n in heav'n his looks & thoughts

Were always downward bent, admiring more

The riches of Heav'ns pavement, trod'n Gold,

Then aught divine or holy else enjoy'd

In vision beatific: by him first

Men also, and by his suggestion taught,

Ransack'd the Center, and with impious hands

Rifl'd the bowels of thir mother Earth

For Treasures better hid. Soon had his crew

Op'nd into the Hill a spacious wound

And dig'd out ribs of Gold. Let none admire

That riches grow in Hell; that soyle may best

Deserve the pretious bane. And here let those

Who boast in mortal things, and wondring tell

Of Babel, and the works of Memphian Kings,

Learn how thir greatest Monuments of Fame,

And Strength and Art are easily outdone

By Spirits reprobate, and in an hour

What in an age they with incessant toyle

And hands innumerable scarce perform

Nigh on the Plain in many cells prepar'd,

That underneath had veins of liquid fire

Sluc'd from the Lake, a second multitude

With wondrous Art founded the massie Ore,

Severing each kinde, and scum'd the Bullion dross:

A third as soon had form'd within the ground

A various mould, and from the boyling cells

By strange conveyance fill'd each hollow nook,

As in an Organ from one blast of wind

To many a row of Pipes the sound-board breaths.

Anon out of the earth a Fabrick huge

Rose like an Exhalation, with the sound

Of Dulcet Symphonies and voices sweet,

Built like a Temple, where Pilasters round

Were set, and Doric pillars overlaid

With Golden Architrave; nor did there want

Cornice or Freeze, with bossy Sculptures grav'n,

The Roof was fretted Gold. Not Babilon,

Nor great Alcairo such magnificence

Equal'd in all thir glories, to inshrine

Belus or Serapis thir Gods, or seat

Thir Kings, when Aegypt with Assyria strove

In wealth and luxurie. Th' ascending pile

Stood fixt her stately highth, and strait the dores
Op'ning thir brazen foulds discover wide
Within, her ample spaces, o're the smooth
And level pavement: from the arched roof
Pendant by suttle Magic many a row
Of Starry Lamps and blazing Cressets fed
With Naphtha and Asphaltus yeilded light
As from a sky. The hasty multitude
Admiring enter'd, and the work some praise
And some the Architect: his hand was known
In Heav'n by many a Towred structure high,
Where Scepter'd Angels held thir residence,
And sat as Princes, whom the supreme King
Exalted to such power, and gave to rule,
Each in his Herarchie, the Orders bright.
Nor was his name unheard or unador'd
In ancient Greece; and in Ausonian land
Men call'd him Mulciber; and how he fell
From Heav'n, they fabl'd, thrown by angry Jove
Sheer o're the Chrystal Battlements: from Morn
To Noon he fell, from Noon to dewy Eve,
A Summers day; and with the setting Sun
Dropt from the Zenith like a falling Star,
On Lemnos th' Aegaean Ile: thus they relate,
Erring; for he with this rebellious rout
Fell long before; nor aught avail'd him now
To have built in Heav'n high Towrs; nor did he scape

By all his Engins, but was headlong sent

With his industrious crew to build in hell.

Mean while the winged Haralds by command

Of Sovran power, with awful Ceremony

And Trumpets sound throughout the Host proclaim

A solemn Councel forthwith to be held

At Pandaemonium, the high Capital

Of Satan and his Peers: thir summons call'd

From every and Band squared Regiment

By place or choice the worthiest; they anon

With hundreds and with thousands trooping came

Attended: all access was throng'd, the Gates

And Porches wide, but chief the spacious Hall

(Though like a cover'd field, where Champions bold

Wont ride in arm'd, and at the Soldans chair

Defi'd the best of Panim chivalry

To mortal combat or carreer with Lance)

Thick swarm'd, both on the ground and in the air,

Brusht with the hiss of russling wings. As Bees

In spring time, when the Sun with Taurus rides,

Poure forth thir populous youth about the Hive

In clusters; they among fresh dews and flowers

Flie to and fro, or on the smoothed Plank,

The suburb of thir Straw-built Cittadel,

New rub'd with Baume, expatiate and confer

Thir State affairs. So thick the aerie crowd

Swarm'd and were straitn'd; till the Signal giv'n,

Behold a wonder! they but now who seemd

In bigness to surpass Earths Giant Sons

Now less then smallest Dwarfs, in narrow room

Throng numberless, like that Pigmean Race

Beyond the Indian Mount, or Faerie Elves,

Whose midnight Revels, by a Forrest side

Or Fountain fome belated Peasant sees,

Or dreams he sees, while over head the Moon

Sits Arbitress, and neerer to the Earth

Wheels her pale course, they on thir mirth & dance

Intent, with jocond Music charm his ear;

At once with joy and fear his heart rebounds.

Thus incorporeal Spirits to smallest forms

Reduc'd thir shapes immense, and were at large,

Though without number still amidst the Hall

Of that infernal Court. But far within

And in thir own dimensions like themselves

The great Seraphic Lords and Cherubim

In close recess and secret conclave sat

A thousand Demy-Gods on golden seat's,

Frequent and full. After short silence then

And summons read, the great consult began.

THE END OF THE FIRST BOOK